Traudl & Walter Reiner

# FITNESS FOR

# CATS

VICTOR GOLLANCZ

LONDON

First published in Great Britain 1993
by Victor Gollancz
an imprint of Cassell
Villiers House, 41/47 Strand, London WC2N 5JE

© by Traudl & Walter Reiner and Wilhelm Heyne Verlag GmbH & Co.
KG, München 1992

English translation copyright © 1993 Victor Gollancz

A catalogue record for this book is
available from the British Library

ISBN 0 575 05396 8

Printed in Italy by New Interlitho SpA, Milan

*For Fluffy, Mew-Mew, Jackie
and all feline fitness freaks*

MENS SANA IN
CORPORE SANO*

*A healthy cat in a healthy coat

Felix

May Ling

Scrappy

Sir Henry

Blackie

Whiskers

We would like to thank
Arnie Schwarzencatter and
the trainers at the gym for
their help and advice.
*The Feline Fitness Club*

## *Warming up*
### Forward trunk twist

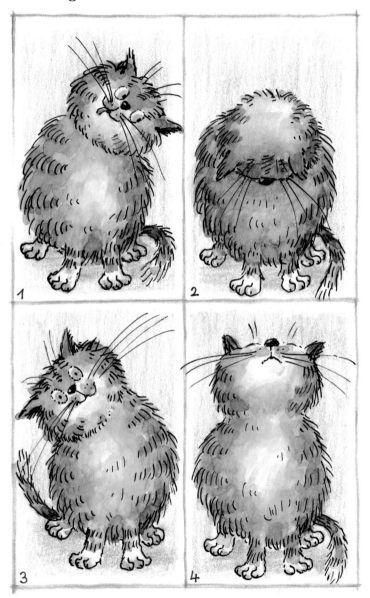

**_Sideways bending:_** this movement stretches the tummy muscles and the lateral oblique muscles, otherwise known as your sides

***The lunge:*** an exercise for the front thigh muscles (the
quadriceps femoris)

### *Trunk bending with knees straight*

Strengthens the muscles of the lower back

# Free exercise routine (without apparatus)

### The windmill
For sinews, ligaments, muscles and joints

### The backwards roll
Breathe in as you rock back and out as you roll forward

### *The standing bend*

- increases blood supply to the head and even helps prevent wrinkles
- is good for the digestion

### *Mountain and valley*

- is good for the back
- develops the chest muscles
- firms and slims the bottom

## The bridge

- stretches and firms the upper thighs, hips and stomach
- relaxes tension
- strengthens the back and legs

## *Deep knee bends*

- exercise the knee and hip joints
- help prevent varicose veins
- tone and massage the muscles of the hips and buttocks; good for the feline figure

1

2

## Super trampolining

- massages the heart
- tones up the entire nervous system
- strengthens the stomach muscles and internal organs
- gives a feeling of vitality

## Leg flexing (with a partner)

Strengthens friendships and
leg-stretching muscles

### The forward lean

To strengthen the back thigh muscles

### *Leg flexing (variant)*
Improves the fitness of the
leg-stretching muscles

1

2

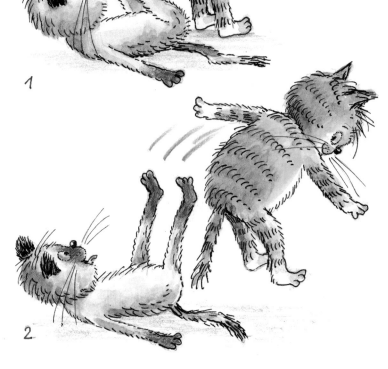

## The catapult

An exercise to improve the strength and reflexes of the leg muscles, as well as those special cat-landings

1

2

### *Sit-ups*
To strengthen the abdominal muscles

***Trunk bending***
To stretch the back
muscles of the thighs,
bottom and back

1

2

## Intensive sit-ups

To strengthen the oblique abdominal muscles even more

To strengthen the
arm and shoulder
muscles

## *Swimming*

Exercises the heart, the circulation and the muscular system especially the fishing muscles

### *Snatch and lift (with long dumb-bells)*

Develops the strength and size of the shoulder muscles
(the deltoids), and of the back and the triceps.
No slippery paws here

Bring the dumb-bells to
shoulder height, then lift
them above your head . . .

. . . until your arms are perfectly straight! Hold the weights steady . . .

. . . without letting them sway backwards or forwards . . .

You need good technique to exercise with weights

## *The twist*

Exercises the lateral
muscles of the trunk

## *Expander exercise*

Strengthens the chest muscles
(the pectoralis major) and the
triceps and deltoids

## *Leg lifts, lying prone*

Muscles exercised: gluteus maximus,
adductor magnus, biceps (of the leg),
erector spinae

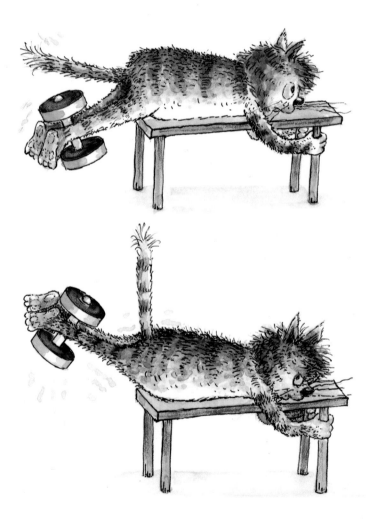

### *Two-handed backwards throw with short dumb-bell*

– checking what's behind you first

Muscles exercised: latissimus
teres major, rectus abdominis,
pectoralis, triceps

### *Dumb-bell exercise (sitting)*

To develop the biceps
(of the arms) and deltoid
muscles

### *Dumb-bell exercise (lying)*

Muscles exercised:
pectoral, biceps,
coracobrachialis,
deltoideus anterior

### *Pull-ups*

Muscles exercised: biceps,
triceps, latissimus pectoralis,
subscapularis, deltoideus posterior

### *Knee bends with side flexing*

Muscles exercised: latissimus rhomboideus
major and minor, trapezius transversalis,
pectoralis, triceps

## *Cycling*

Exercises the heart, lungs and muscles. Cycling is good exercise for both strength and stamina. But watch those tails!

### Home exercise cycle, for heart and circulation

Shows calorie consumption, training time and 'distance', speed, pedalling rhythm, and pulse frequency with warning bleep!

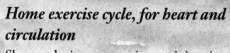

### *Stepping machine*

Shows training time, stepping
handicap, calorie consumption,
speed, muscle toning

## *Hyper-extension*

Exercise for the back
and hip muscles

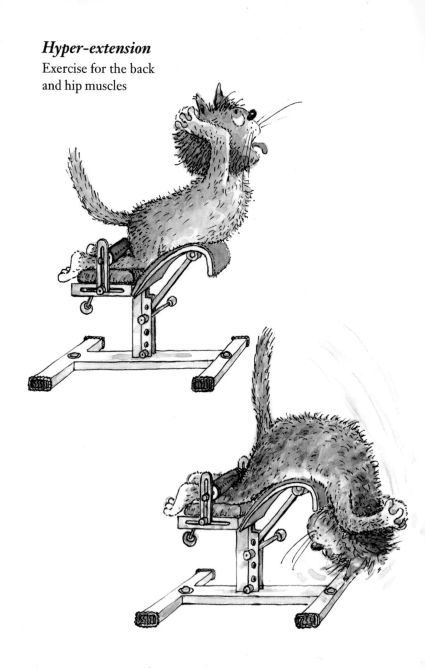

## *Exercising the abdominal muscles*

Good for flattening
the tummy

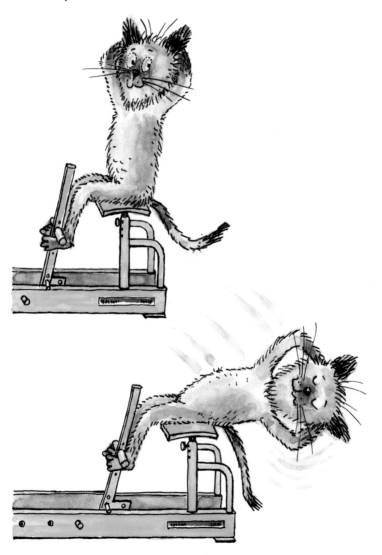

## Rowing machine

Exercises the muscles of legs, stomach and arms. Electronic indicator shows training time, stroke rate and speed handicap

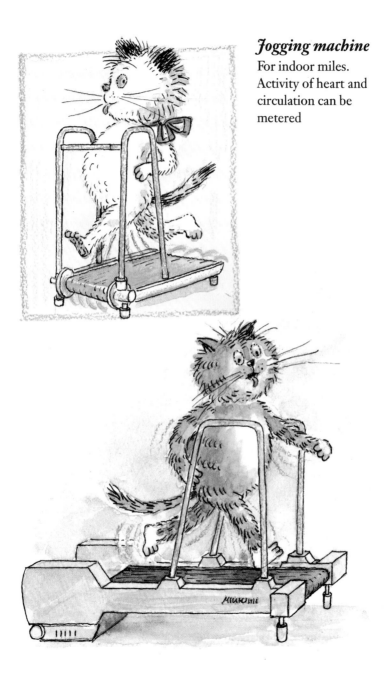

### *Jogging machine*
For indoor miles.
Activity of heart and
circulation can be
metered

### *Running*

Good for the heart, brain, liver,
kidneys, arteries, skin and fur

### *Downward bar-pull, paws close together*

Exercises the muscles connecting the arm to the body

Muscles exercised:
  biceps
  triceps
  latissimus
  teres major
  pectoralis
  subscapularis
  deltoideus posterior

***Downward bar-pull,***
***paws apart***
(Keep the paws out to the side)

Muscles exercised:
   latissimus
   rhomboideus
   trapezius transversalis
   teres major and minor
   pectoralis
   triceps
   biceps

## *Underarm trainer*

Specially for tennis
players and golfers

Strengthens the underarm
muscles and wrist sinews.
Good for your tennis serve

### *Training with dumb-bells*
Tones the abdominal muscles and main back muscle

## *Rowing machine*

Exercises the entire body

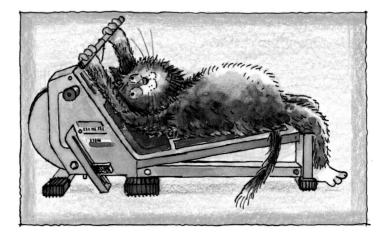

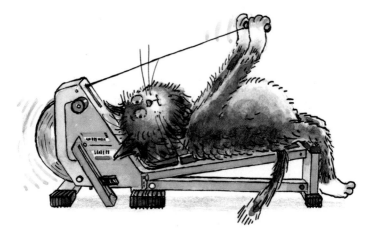

### *Stomach tightening*

Pulling the bars towards you
strengthens the muscles of
the side and lower back

## *Neck pressure exercise*
Strengthens the shoulder muscles

## *Weight-shifting*

Exercises the muscles of the chest
and arms. Press arms smoothly
forward, return to starting position

Muscles exercised:
    pectoralis
    coracobrachialis
    deltoideus anterior

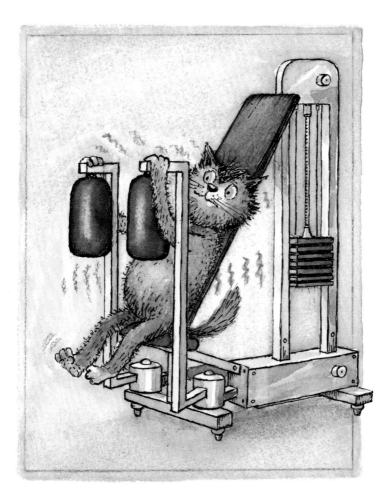

# Leg flexing
To firm up the buttocks

1

Push the pedals rhythmically until the legs are fully stretched, then return slowly to starting position. Don't forget to breathe out as you exert pressure

### *Jazz dancing*

Self-expression in dance enhances personal development.
The rhythm, attitudes and movements of dancing are good
for general physical fitness. A chance to miaow along, too

# Heel raising

Trains the muscles of
the hips and upper
thighs

Muscles exercised:
serratus anterior
trapezius
deltoideus
triceps

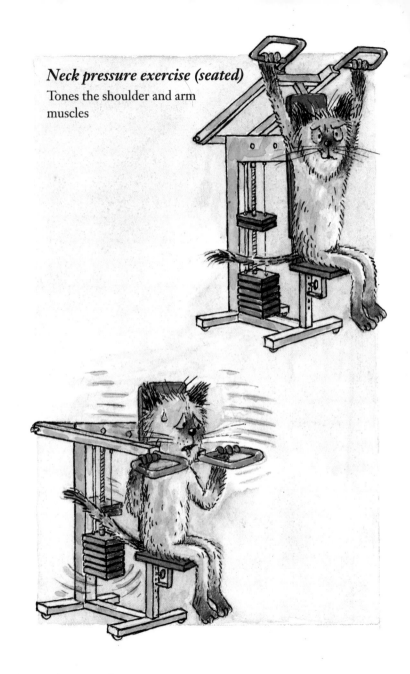

***Neck pressure exercise (seated)***

Tones the shoulder and arm muscles

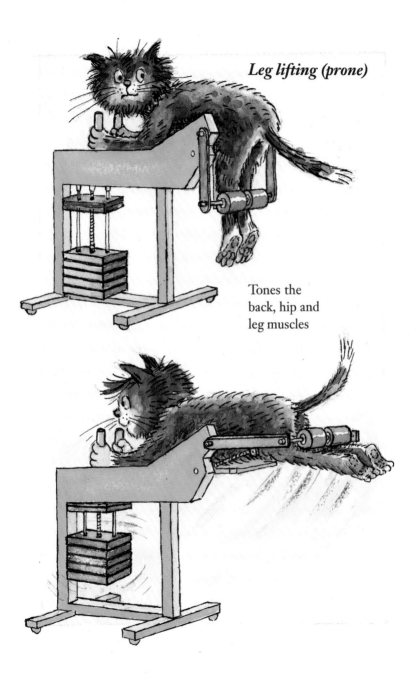

*Leg lifting (prone)*

Tones the
back, hip and
leg muscles

### *Back stretching*

Exercises the spine, hip
joints, stomach muscles,
iliac muscles and loin
muscles

### *Arms out and up (with apparatus)*

Exercises the shoulder joints, shoulder-blades, collarbone joint, upper back muscles, serratus and trapezius

## *Cooling down*

Trunk bending is the best way to finish an exercise session

### *Thigh stretching*
Tones the thigh muscles (quadriceps femoris)

## *Sideways bends, seated*
Do twenty each side

### *Trunk bends, seated*

Your knee sinews, lower back and the muscles of your trunk will
be well loosened up by now – these trunk bends
are ideal for ending
an exercise session

### *A balanced diet helps fitness!*

- Eat less, exercise more
- Protein, carbohydrate and fat are important.

Fish and milk are good, but avoid the cream!

## A proper diet
### Calorie consumption in relation to body weight*

| Body weight in kilos | light exercise cals | medium exercise cals | heavy exercise cals |
| --- | --- | --- | --- |
| 6.00 | 195 | 225 | 300 |
| 6.5 | 210 | 240 | 325 |
| 7.00 | 225 | 260 | 350 |
| 7.5 | 240 | 280 | 375 |
| 8.00 | 260 | 300 | 400 |
| 8.5 | 275 | 315 | 425 |
| 9.00 | 290 | 330 | 450 |

*Published by the Feline Dietary Association

Double biceps pose, from front

Muscle-man pose

Biceps pose, paw behind neck

Sideways biceps pose

### *Practice posing this way!*

Take as much care over posing as any other aspect of training. You'll need a full-length mirror for these exercises – and put everything you've got into them!

Stomach muscle pose, arms raised

These standard poses have been selected by the International Federation of Bodybuilders (IFBB)

Stomach muscle pose, arms front

If your cat has any puff left, it will love the other two books in this delightful series:

YOGA FOR CATS
ISBN 0 575 05122 1 · £4.99

ASTROLOGY FOR CATS
ISBN 0 575 05348 8 · £4.99

Available from Victor Gollancz

*Fitness For Cats*